MICHAEL GOODMAN

KENDALL ELEMENTARY SCHOOL
2408 MEADOW LAKE DR.
NAPERVILLE, IL 60564

CREATIVE 🍎 EDUCATION

Published by Creative Education
123 South Broad Street, Mankato, Minnesota 56001
Creative Education is an imprint of The Creative Company

Designed by Rita Marshall
Cover illustration by Rob Day

Photos by: Allsport Photography, Associated Press, Bettmann Archive,
Duomo, Focus on Sports, Fotosport, Spectra Action, and SportsChrome.

Library of Congress Cataloging-in-Publication Data

Goodman, Michael E.
Chicago Bears / by Michael Goodman.
p. cm. — (NFL Today)
Summary: Traces the history of the team from its beginnings through 1996.
ISBN 0-88682-792-2

1. Chicago Bears (Football team)—History—Juvenile literature.
[1. Chicago Bears (Football team) 2. Football—History.]
I. Title. II. Series.

GV956.C5G66   1996   96-15232
796.332'64'0977311--dc20

October 16, 1921, was like many other Sundays in Chicago, Illinois. It was a beautiful autumn afternoon in the city on Lake Michigan's southern shore. Most families were enjoying a break from what was then a six-day work week. But one young man in Chicago was too busy and nervous to relax.

George Halas, a 26-year-old athlete and entrepreneur, planned to introduce his professional football team, the Chicago Bears, to the people of the Windy City that afternoon. The contest was to be played at Cubs Park (the future Wrigley Field), and the cost of a ticket was one dollar.

"Papa Bear" George Halas (far right).

Future Bears coach, Paddy Driscoll excelled at running, punting and drop-kicking field goals as a Bears running back.

Halas and his partner Dutch Sternaman had paid $100 each to the Staley Starch Company in nearby Decatur to purchase its semi-pro team, the Decatur Staleys. They renamed the team the Bears and moved it to Chicago. The two men hoped that enough tickets would be sold to cover expenses and earn back their investment. Arriving by streetcar, by Model-T and on foot, nearly 8,000 spectators came out on that first Sunday afternoon to cheer for the team in midnight blue and orange. It was a rousing start.

Those fans could not have guessed that the fledgling Bears would, over the next 75 years, win nearly 600 games, capture eight National Football League championships—plus one Super Bowl—and secure berths in the Pro Football Hall of Fame for a record 23 team members, including Halas himself.

PAPA BEAR

Throughout the club's history, the Chicago Bears have been more than a team. They have been a family, held together for their first 60 years by "Papa Bear," George Halas. Halas soon took over sole ownership of the team. In its early days, he would also sell tickets, tape ankles, shovel snow, coach and occasionally play defense. In one game against the Oorang Indians, led by the legendary Jim Thorpe, Halas put himself in at defensive end, recovered a Thorpe fumble and raced 98 yards for a Chicago touchdown.

Halas served as the Bears coach for four separate stints between 1921 and 1967. He won NFL championships at age 26 and at age 68, and the 40 different teams he coached finished below

Stellar running back, Neal Anderson (page 7).

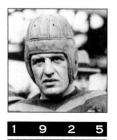

Big Bucks! Red Grange signed a contract with the Bears for the astronomical sum of $100,000!

.500 only six times. Halas was a man of many firsts. He was the first NFL coach to schedule daily practices, the first to study game films, the first to scout small colleges for talent and the first to introduce a team song. But above all, Halas was the first man to dream that football could become a first-class, big-league sport.

Halas' dreams for professional football in Chicago might not have come true if he had not recruited two exceptional running backs—Red Grange and Bronko Nagurski.

Grange, known as "the Galloping Ghost," signed with the Bears on November 22, 1925, after a legendary career at the University of Illinois. In those days, college football was big news in America, while pro football seldom made the headlines. Grange would change all of that. The Bears began an amazing cross-country tour on Thanksgiving Day in 1925, playing 19 games in 66 days, including eight in a 12-day period. "Those 66 days made professional football," *Sports Illustrated* magazine later noted. In one game in New York's Polo Grounds, a record 73,000 people turned out to see Grange and his teammates defeat the Giants 19-7, the beginning of a major rivalry between those two clubs.

Grange's importance to the Bears extended past 1925. He anchored the club throughout its early years, caught the winning pass in the 1932 NFL championship game and made a tackle at the end of the 1933 title game that saved that contest for Chicago.

During the 1930 season, Grange was joined in the Bear backfield by a bruising competitor named Bronislau Nagurski. Better known as "Bronko," this unstoppable force played for the Bears until 1937, then came out of retirement for a final year in 1943 at Halas' request. Nagurski's bone-jarring runs were his trademark. In one game, he blasted through two tacklers, raced across the end zone and ran full speed into a brick retaining wall behind it. Shaking his head, which was covered by a flimsy leather helmet, Nagurski trotted back to the bench and remarked, "That last guy really gave me a good lick."

Running back Bronko Nagurski pounded out 529 yards rushing during the season.

Not many things could stop Chicago in the early 1930s. In 1932, Grange and Nagurski combined for one of the greatest moments in Bears history. During the championship game against the Portsmouth Spartans, the game was scoreless in the fourth quarter. The Bears got the ball back and began driving, feeding Bronko the ball on almost every play. On fourth-and-goal from the two, Bronko took the ball once again and saw that a wall of Portsmouth tacklers awaited him. So he stopped short, leaped up and tossed a short pass to Grange for the winning touchdown.

The two Bears stars teamed up to lead Chicago to a second consecutive championship in 1933 and to the title game in 1934. Through the remainder of the 1930s, the brilliance faded and Nagurski and Grange became battered veterans. Though Father Time finally caught up with them, the Galloping Ghost and Bronko were both ultimately enshrined in the Hall of Fame.

LUCKY WITH LUCKMAN

With Chicago's legends at the end of their careers, Halas needed someone to lead the Bears back to the top. In 1939, Papa Bear drafted a tailback from Columbia named Sid Luckman and transformed him from a runner to a passer. With Luckman at quarterback, a new Bears dynasty began.

Dan Hampton (#99) and Richard Dent (#95) (pages 10-11).

KENDALL ELEMENTARY SCHOOL
2408 MEADOW LAKE DR.
NAPERVILLE, IL 60564

From 1940 to 1943, Luckman led the Bears to an incredible 37-5-1 record, four Western Division titles, and three NFL championships. Luckman and other Bears stars such as Bulldog Turner, George McAfee and Joe Stydahar (all future Hall of Famers) played some outstanding football games during those four seasons, but no contest came as close to perfection as the 1940 NFL championship game against the Washington Redskins. To add to the excitement, that game was the first ever broadcast to a national radio audience.

Just three weeks earlier, Washington had knocked off the Bears 7-3 on a controversial call. When the Bears complained, Washington owner George Marshall told the press that "the Bears were quitters and a bunch of cry babies."

Halas was furious. He took the press clippings and plastered them on the locker room walls. Then he gave the team an inspir-

ing pep talk. He ended by saying, "Gentlemen, this is what the Redskins think of you. I think you're a great football team, the greatest ever assembled. Go out onto the field and prove it."

Spurred on by pride and anger, the Bears walloped Washington 73-0 in the most lopsided pro football game of all time. It got so bad that, at one point, the referees approached Halas and asked if he would try not to kick any more extra points. So many balls had been booted into the stands and kept by the fans as souvenirs that the Redskins were down to their last football.

"Some observers said the Bears were a perfect football team that day," recalled Halas. "I can't agree. Looking over the movies, I can see where we should have scored another touchdown."

Sid Luckman's Chicago dynasty was slowed down by World War II, as many top players left to join the armed forces. The club resumed its winning ways with an NFL championship in 1946 and some fine plays throughout the rest of the decade. Luckman's retirement after the 1951 season marked the end of the second golden era in Bears history.

The Bears' fortunes took a downward turn during the rest of the 1950s. Still, the teams of those years featured some exceptional talent. Running backs Rick Casares and Willie Gallimore excited fans with their speed and power; quarterbacks Ed Brown and Bill Wade were solid leaders; Johnny Morris and Harlon Hill were outstanding receivers; and no one was tougher than middle linebacker Bill George. Still, something was missing.

George Halas, who had given up head coaching duties in the mid-1950s, decided that the team needed him back at the controls in 1958. Sure enough, the Bears began edging their way back up the NFL standings. By 1963, Halas and his right-

1 9 4 3

Sid Luckman became the first professional quarterback to pass for over 400 yards in a game.

Quarterback Bill Wade (#9) could stay cool under pressure.

hand man, defensive coordinator George Allen, directed the Bears back to the NFL championship game against their arch rivals, the New York Giants. The Giants, led by quarterback Y.A. Tittle and running back Frank Gifford, were heavy favorites. But Allen's defenders shut down the vaunted New York offense, intercepting five Tittle passes on the way to a 14-10 upset victory. The NFL championship trophy was back in Chicago after a 17-year absence.

TWO OF THE BEST

The Bears didn't stay on top for long, but the team did soon acquire two special stars—Dick Butkus and Gale Sayers—who would excite Windy City fans for years. Halas selected

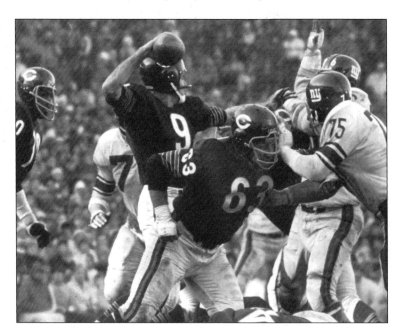

Linebacker Dick Butkus.

both players in the 1965 college draft, and they quickly became legends.

Dick Butkus was a dominant defensive force, but there was nothing pretty about the way he played. He was notorious for his hard hitting. "Butkus was the epitome of the middle linebacker," said Mike Ditka, a teammate for several years. "He played the game from the tip of his head to the bottom of his soles."

Before Butkus came along, most kids wanted to be offensive stars. Once they watched him in action, the toughest ones wanted to play defense—just like Dick Butkus.

If Butkus represented brute strength on the field, Gale Sayers epitomized gracefulness. He had speed, finesse and power, too, when he needed it. He was an outstanding rusher, receiver, and kick returner—perhaps the best all-around offensive star

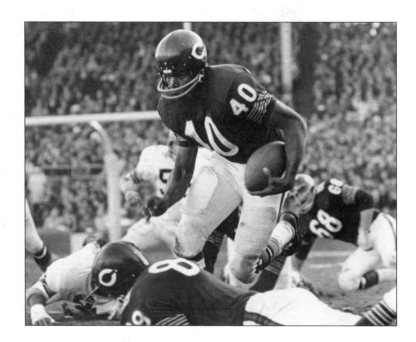

Mike Ditka made many acrobatic catches in 1966.

in NFL history. During one game against the San Francisco 49ers, rookie Sayers scored a remarkable six touchdowns—one on a pass, two on speedy end sweeps, two on power dives up the middle and the last on an 85-yard zigzagging punt return.

"He's no different from any other runner when he's coming at you," noted a 49er, "but when he gets there he's gone."

Bad knees forced Sayers into early retirement in 1971, but six years later he was elected to the Hall of Fame at age 34, the youngest member ever. Butkus, who retired after the 1973 season, joined Sayers in the Hall of Fame in 1979.

Wally Chambers, the Bears first round pick in 1973, went on to three Pro Bowl appearances at defensive tackle.

SWEETNESS

In the decade between 1966 and 1975, the Bears had only one winning season. But the last year of that losing streak

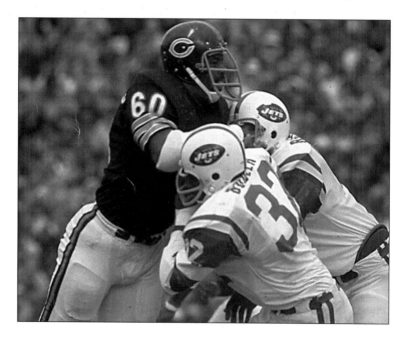

also marked the arrival of the next great player in Chicago, Walter Payton.

Walter Jerry Payton was born and raised in Columbia, Mississippi. He spent most of his childhood living in the shadow of his older brother, Eddie, who also played in the NFL. In high school, Walter didn't go out for the football team until after Eddie had graduated. Instead, he played drums in the band and joined the gymnastics team. Once he got to the football field, however, Walter was a natural. He ran for a 61-yard touchdown in his first high school game. After an outstanding college career at Jackson State in Mississippi, Payton continued his excellence as a professional.

1 9 8 3

Gale Sayers' record rushing yards of 1,032 was topped by Walter Payton in 1983 (1,421).

"Sweetness," Payton's nickname, was tough on opposing defenders. In fitting with Bear's tradition, Payton loved hard-nosed play. In his 10th season in Chicago, Payton was nearing Jim Brown's NFL career rushing record of 12,312 yards. A reporter asked Payton how he would like to break the mark. Payton replied, "I want to go up the middle, hit one guy, bounce off, hit another, jump over someone and fight for the extra yard." Payton not only surpassed Brown's record, he shattered it, completing his career in 1987 with 16,726 yards rushing.

The shy and quiet Payton always gave credit to his linemen and presented each of them with an engraved gold watch after he broke Brown's mark in 1984. But what Payton and his teammates really wanted was a Super Bowl ring.

THE DITKA YEARS

George Halas also longed for a championship ring. Though he felt he was too old to coach the Bears to victory again, he knew the right man for the job—a tough, former Bears tight

Walter Payton holds eight NFL records.

end named Mike Ditka. Ditka had played on the last Chicago championship club in 1963. During six seasons in Chicago, Ditka caught more than 300 passes for over 4,500 yards to place among the all-time team leaders. He also threw some devastating blocks to protect his quarterback or to open a hole for a Bears runner. Known as "Iron Mike," he was emotional, maybe even hotheaded and intimidating, but he knew how to win and how to inspire others to want to win. Best of all, he bled navy blue, orange and white (the Bears' colors). "I was always a Bear," admitted Ditka. "Even when I was playing and coaching in Dallas, I was a Chicago Bear."

Coach Mike Ditka guided the Bears to their first of five consecutive Central Division titles.

Ditka had a wealth of talent awaiting him when he came back to Chicago before the 1982 season. The defense was anchored by standout end Dan Hampton, linebacker Mike Singletary and safety Gary Fencik. On offense, there was Payton, plus a rookie quarterback from Brigham Young University named Jim McMahon. Ditka's job was to take these thoroughbreds to the race and win.

Unfortunately, George Halas would not be there in the winner's circle. Papa Bear died of a heart attack on October 31, 1983. The Bears' owner for 62 years was also one of the greatest coaches in NFL history—with a career record of 326-151-31—and the Bears' biggest fan. He would be sorely missed.

Wearing black bands with the initials GSH on their sleeves to honor Halas' memory, Ditka's Bears clawed their way to .500 at 8-8 in 1983, then captured the NFC Central Division title in 1984 with a 10-6 record. Walter Payton contributed 1,684 rushing yards that year to key the offense, but it was Ditka's defense that led the way. The Bear defenders were practically impenetrable. They overcame the powerful Washington Redskins for a 23-19 first-round playoff win, but were unable to halt the San Francisco 49ers in the NFC title game. The 49ers went on to

Left to right: William Perry, Dan Hampton, Richard Dent, Mike Singletary.

capture the Super Bowl in 1984, but Bears players and fans were certain that their time on top would come soon.

Soon turned out to be the following year. The Bears won their first 12 games in 1985 en route to a stellar 15-1 record. Once again, the key was the defense. Five Chicago defenders were named All-Pros that year, with tackle Richard Dent leading the league in sacks and linebacker Mike Singletary being named United Press International's Defensive Player of the Year. The defense also featured a 320-pound rookie named William Perry, whose nickname, "the Refrigerator," referred either to his size or to his favorite place in the house. Perry, a defensive tackle, even played fullback on occasion, when the Bears wanted a "really big" blocker or runner in the game. On offense, Payton gained 1,551 yards and McMahon threw for 2,392 more. The team was poised to help Sweetness win his Super Bowl ring.

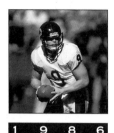

1 9 8 6

Super Bowl, Super Play: Quarterback Jim McMahon passed for 250 yards and rushed for two touchdowns.

They did just that—in amazing fashion. First the Bear defenders shut down the New York Giants 21-0 to propel the team to the 1985 NFC championship game against the Los Angeles Rams. The fearsome Bears defense again shut the door on the Rams while McMahon led the Chicago offense to a 24-0, and its first Super Bowl berth.

In Super Bowl XX, Chicago's shutout streak ended when the New England Patriots scored on a first-period field goal to go up 3-0, but that lead was short-lived. Chicago scored the next 44 points on the way to a 46-10 rout that was almost as one-sided as the Bears' 73-0 triumph over the Redskins 45 years earlier. Mike Ditka and the Bears were the "toast of the town" in Chicago once again.

The Bears continued to dominate the NFC's Central Division from 1986 through 1988, winning their third, fourth and fifth

Alonzo Spellman smothers a Lion (pages 26-27).

Defensive tackle Jim Flanigan doubled as an offensive fullback.

consecutive division titles and earning playoff berths each year. During that five-year span, the Bears won a total of 62 games, the most ever by an NFL squad. However, Chicago fell to the Redskins in the postseason in both 1986 and 1987 and to the 49ers in 1988 in the NFC championship game.

The late 1980s saw the emergence of several new Bears stars, as many of the old guards retired or were traded. Payton stripped down in 1987 and was ultimately elected to the Hall of Fame in 1993. But his replacement at running back, Neal Anderson, rushed for 1,000 yards three years in a row. Anderson was also the team's leading receiver. Mike Tomczak and Jim Harbaugh shared quarterbacking duties in place of Jim McMahon, and new defensive standouts included Dave Duerson, Trace Armstrong and Steve McMichael.

After a disappointing 6-10 campaign in 1989, the Bears bounced back with 11-5 seasons in both 1990 and 1991, helping Mike Ditka to become the only Chicago coach besides George Halas to record 100 victories. But after a 5-11 campaign in 1992, Bear management decided that Ditka's blend of emotion and intimidation was no longer what the club needed.

Before the 1993 season, Dave Wannstedt, who had built the Dallas Cowboys defense into one of the league's best in the early 1990s, was hired to reconstruct the Bears. And he began doing just that, releasing a number of veterans, including Neal Anderson and Richard Dent.

As a result, Wannstedt's first Bears squads did not have many stars. Most of the top players were either young and inexperienced—like defensive lineman Alonzo Spellman and receiver Curtis Conway—or free agents looking for an opportunity to prove themselves. The latter included running back Lewis Tillman, who came from the Giants, and quarterback Eric Kramer, a former Detroit Lion. Wannstedt convinced these players that they could be winners.

"The main idea behind Dave's coaching philosophy is to keep a positive mental attitude," said Bears center Jerry Fontenot. "We don't focus on why we lost. We don't point fingers. We focus on what we have to do to win."

By 1994, Wannstedt's philosophy began to take hold. The rejuvenated Bears defied the experts by finishing 9-7 and then trouncing the division champion Minnesota Vikings 35-18 in the first round playoffs. Their bubble finally burst when San Francisco crushed them 44-15 on the way to a 49ers Super Bowl title.

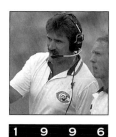

1 9 9 6

After only a short time, Coach Wannstedt has established himself among the NFL's elite.

Following the loss to the 49ers, Wannstedt apologized to Chicago fans and promised that the coaches and team would begin working even harder the next year.

The coaching squad began its work during the 1995 college draft. To bolster the club's offensive game, Wannstedt added Heismann Trophy winner Rashaam Salaam from the University of Colorado. Salaam gained over 2,000 yards rushing in his senior year, and he lived up to expectations as the NFL's top rookie rusher in 1995. By season's end, Salaam had accumulated 1,074 yards on the ground, eighth-best overall in the conference. Wannstedt also selected big, speedy defensive tackle Pat Riley from the collegiate powerhouse Miami Hurricanes to fortify the team's defensive line.

Then during the 1995 pre-season, Wannstedt made a key decision, picking Erik Kramer to replace Steve Walsh as the Bears' starting quarterback. Kramer's stronger arm enabled the Bears to establish a long passing game featuring speedy wide receivers Jeff Graham and Curtis Conway. By season's end, Kramer had rewritten team record books with 315 completions for 3,838

Sensational Rashaam Salaam was the youngest player in the NFL in 1995.

Quarterback Erik Kramer emerged as a star in 1995.　　　31

yards and 29 touchdowns. The 29 scoring strikes broke Sid Luckman's club record of 28 established in 1943.

The Bears' improved passing attack, coupled with Salaam's running, helped Chicago move back near the top of the NFC Central Division with a 9-7 record. The Bears seemed headed for the playoffs, but they were edged out for the final Wild Card spot by Atlanta. Chicago fans were a little disappointed, but they didn't feel Wannstedt owed them another apology. After all, the "new" offensive-minded Bears had become one of the most entertaining clubs in the league.

Quarterback Kramer emphasized, at season's end, that the team's strength gave the Bears hope for the future. "There were a lot of negative things going on," Kramer said. "It was very stressful. But we played well and we stayed in contention."

It has been more than 75 years since that fateful Sunday afternoon when George Halas first presented his Chicago Bears team to fans in the Windy City. On that day, Bears fans knew—and continue to believe—that a winner was in the making. The "Monsters of the Midway" are on their way back to the top.

1 9 9 7

Former Dolphin Bryan Cox brought his hard-nosed tackling to the Bears.